MICROLIFE

Fighting Infectious Diseases

Revised and Updated

Robert Snedden

Heinemann Library
Chicago, Illinois

Customer Service 888-454-2279
Visit our website at www.heinemannraintree.com

Editorial: Clare Lewis
Design: Joanna Hinton-Malivoire
Picture Research: Ruth Blair
Production: Sevy Ribierre
Originated by Chroma Graphics Pte. Ltd.
Printed and bound in China by Leo Paper Group

11 10 09 08 07
10 9 8 7 6 5 4 3 2 1

New edition ISBN: 978-1-403-49560-0 (hardcover)
                         978-1-403-49565-5 (paperback)

The Library of Congress has cataloged the first edition as follows:
Snedden, Robert
   Fighting infectious diseases / Robert Snedden.
      p. cm. -- (Microlife)
   Includes bibliographical references and index.
   Summary: Discusses such infectious diseases as rabies, smallpox, AIDS, influenza, and malaria
and describes how they are transmitted and treated.
   ISBN 1-57572-243-7
   1. Communicable diseases -- Juvenile literature. 2. Infection -- Juvenile literature. [1.
Communicable diseases. 2. Diseases] I. Title.
RC112.S62 2000
616.9—dc21
                                                    99-046858

Acknowledgments
The author and publishers are grateful to the following for permission to reproduce copyright
material: Corbis/Mark Rightmire p45, M Schwarz p40; Image Select: p15, N Birch p24, World
Health Organization pp12, 18, 19; Planet Earth Pictures: p31; Science Photo Library: David
Goodsell p9, T Brain p20, BSIP VEM pp7, 37, CNRI p23, J Durham p29, EM Unit, CVL Weybridge
p14, S Fraser p39, A Gragera/Latin Stock p5, M Kage p4, J King-Holmes p42, Dr. K Lounatmaa
pp16, 26 M Meadows/Peter Arnold Inc p17, Moredun Animal Health Ltd p35, S Ogden p41, B Yarvin
p10; Tony Stone Images: Corbis/Rick Gomez p11; Telegraph Colour Library: J Burns p13, Planet Earth/Geof
Du Feu p32, S Rowell p25.

Cover photograph: The *Staphylococcus* bacteria responsible for MRSA is engulfed by a macrophage
or phagocyte. Reproduced with permission of Corbis/Visuals Unlimited.

The publishers would like to thank Dr. Puran Ganeri and Anna Claybourne for their comments in
the preparation of this title.

Some words are shown in bold, **like this.** You can find out what they mean by
looking in the glossary.

Contents

Introduction

It is quite likely that you, or someone else you know, will become sick at some time in the next year. Most of us catch a cold at least once a year. You may remember getting childhood illnesses, such as tonsilitis or chicken pox, or you may remember seeing a younger brother or sister come down with these illnesses. Someone in your family may get flu or, if they are very unlucky, get sick from food poisoning.

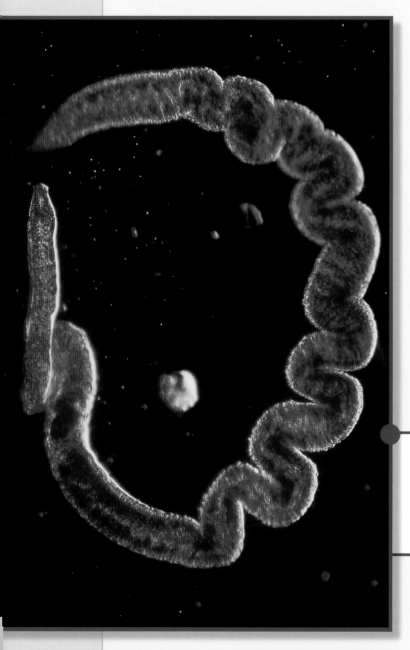

Disease agents

Each of these **infectious** diseases is caused by a particular **microorganism**, an invisibly small life form that can, as the name suggests, only be seen under a microscope. A microorganism that causes infectious illness is called a **disease agent**. From the smallest to the largest, these range from **viruses** to **bacteria, fungi, protists** and **helminths (parasitic worms)**.

An adult female fluke. This parasitic worm causes the disease schistosomiasis, which kills roughly 200,000 people each year.

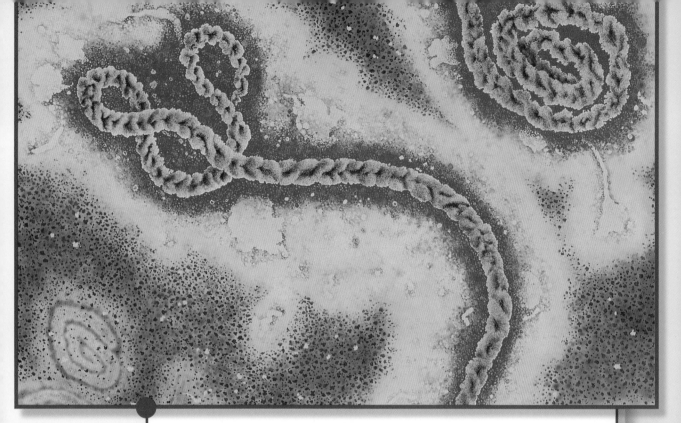

The Ebola virus has been the cause of outbreaks of a particularly severe, and often fatal, fever in parts of Africa in recent years.

The battleground

The number and variety of infectious diseases is formidable. They include malaria, hepatitis, cholera, AIDS, tuberculosis, sleeping sickness, river blindness, Lassa fever, and many more. Some, such as the common cold, are merely inconvenient; others, such as the Ebola virus, are deadly. Some, such as AIDS, are relatively new, while most are as old as humanity. Infectious disease is the leading cause of death each year, causing about one-third of all deaths throughout the world.

In this book we will look at disease agents, the effects they have, and how we can combat them. With so many disease-causing agents all around us, it can sometimes appear astounding that the human race has survived so long. After all, it is only within the last 150 years that the connection between microorganisms and disease has become widely accepted. We will also take a close look at our remarkable **immune system**, the **cells** in our bodies that are dedicated to fighting off micro-invaders, and at the problems we face in dealing with bacteria that are becoming increasingly resistant to our medicines.

Viruses and Vectors

Viruses are simple but effective disease agents. Essentially, a virus is a set of instructions for making a new virus, wrapped up in a protective coat. Viruses are tiny, ranging in size from less than 1 millionth of an inch to 5 millionths of an inch. The period at the end of the last sentence is roughly 2 hundredths of an inch across—so you can figure out how many viruses could fit on it!

Viruses revealed

Although the existence of viruses was suspected by the end of the 1800s, it was not until the electron microscope was perfected after World War Two that people began to see what a virus looked like. Despite their small size, viruses come in a variety of shapes and cause diseases as diverse in their effects and seriousness as AIDS, rabies, polio, measles, influenza, and the common cold.

Viruses themselves are not complete living organisms. They are true parasites, depending entirely on a living organism, called a host, for their needs. No parasite can afford to harm its host too much or to have its host develop an immunity, or resistance, to it. A virus that killed off 100 percent of the people it attacked would soon die out itself when it ran out of new people to infect.

Reservoirs

A successful virus that has severe effects on one host will have another host, called a reservoir host, in which it produces milder effects. This ensures the virus's continued survival. For many human viruses, such as measles, herpes, and influenza, the human population is its own reservoir since different people have different levels of resistance to these diseases.

Disease vectors

The **vector** of a disease is the way in which it gets from one host to another. The transmission of diseases like influenza or herpes comes through the air or through close physical contact.

Other diseases are carried by insects or other animals. Lassa fever, a disease that is often fatal in humans, is transmitted by rodents. Dengue fever, a serious disease of the tropics, is carried by a species of mosquito. Kuru, a 100 percent fatal brain disease found only in New Guinea, was transmitted through a ceremony involving the eating of human brains! Since this habit is no longer followed, the disease—robbed of its vector—is disappearing.

Viruses on the move

In the modern world, people travel more and farther than ever before, using buses, trains, and planes to crisscross the globe. This means that disease vectors are easily carried from one community to another, and diseases can spread much faster than they used to. Governments sometimes stop flights from disease-stricken areas or ask travelers to undergo a health test before they can enter a country, in order to prevent the spread of disease.

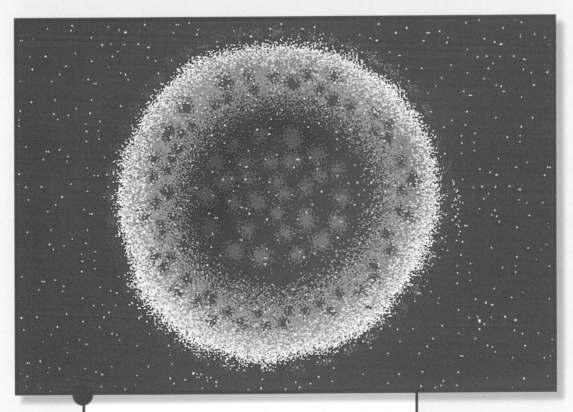

The Lassa fever virus. The virus is carried by rats and can be caught by humans from rat urine, or from droplets coughed into the air by people already infected.

Fighting the Viruses

We are not entirely defenseless against the viruses that try to invade our cells. There are a couple of effective ways in which our bodies can counter virus attacks.

Interferons

If a particular virus infects some of the cells in your body, the infected cells make substances called **interferons**. These are a type of **protein**. Interferons work with cells next to the site of the infection, helping the cells become more resistant to the virus. Sometimes this works, sometimes not. If the resistance is not strong enough, the virus continues to spread and affect more and more cells. The more cells it affects, the sicker we feel.

The immune system

The next line of defense is the body's immune system. It begins to attack the viruses before they can penetrate the cells, and to kill cells that have become infected. Killing the infected cells is somewhat like making a firebreak to keep a forest fire from spreading. A virus needs a living cell in order to reproduce itself, but the immune system kills the cells before the virus has managed to do this. Eventually, if the immune system does its job, the virus will be completely removed from the body and the person will start to feel better.

Antibodies

The body's most effective line of attack against viruses are its **antibodies**, proteins produced by the immune system. Antibodies stop the spread of a disease through the body. The antibody binds onto the virus, making it harmless or destroying it altogether. The body makes large amounts of antibodies when a virus invader is detected. Antibodies are made in places such as the glands under the arm or the tonsils in the throat. This is why some diseases cause sore throats or lumps in the armpits. The glands there are busy pouring antibodies into the bloodstream to fight the virus. Antibodies have no effect against viruses once those viruses get inside cells.

Immunity

Each disease causes the production of a specific antibody to fight it. Some diseases, such as measles, will only make you sick once. This is because the measles antibodies stay in your bloodstream. If measles viruses ever attack again, they are dealt with so swiftly and effectively that you will never know they were there at all. You are said to have become immune to the disease, or developed an immunity.

Antibodies (pink) in the blood are attacking a virus (green and yellow) by binding themselves to its surface.

Immunization

We can produce resistance to a disease without actually catching it. This is done by introducing a **vaccine** into the body.

Vaccines

A vaccine is a weakened or milder form of a virus. It will activate the body's production of antibodies but will not cause any disease **symptoms**. The presence of the antibodies gives immunity against the normal form of the virus. The process of giving immunity in this way is called **immunization**.

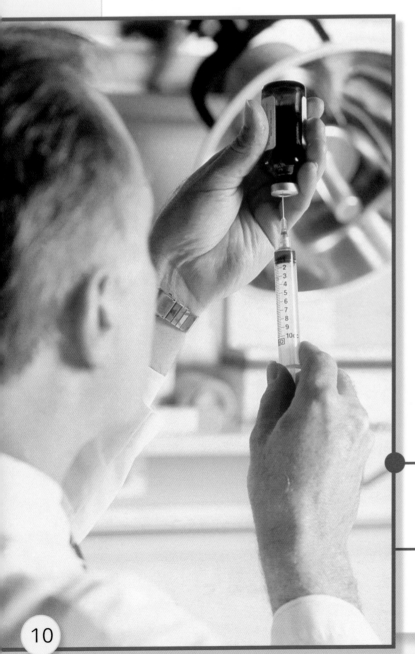

Another method is to use viruses that have been rendered inactive, such as by treating them with the chemical formaldehyde. These viruses are then introduced into the body as a "killed" vaccine. Although the virus is inactive, the immune system can still recognize it and is triggered to produce antibodies.

A hypodermic syringe is often used to give accurately measured doses of vaccines.

Passive immunization

Passive immunization means the person being immunized is not involved in making antibodies. Instead, an animal, such as a horse, is immunized. The antibodies that the horse produces are collected from its blood and purified. They are then injected into the human. The result is that the human acquires immediate immunity to the disease. Immunity acquired in this way is only temporary, however, as the body is not stimulated into making its own antibodies.

Mother and baby

Passive immunity occurs naturally when antibodies are transferred from the mother to the fetus through the placenta. A baby also gets antibodies through colostrum, which is found in breast milk.

Vaccination

Vaccination is generally given by an injection (shot), whatever the virus's natural route into the body might be. An exception to this is live polio vaccine, which is given orally (by mouth), the virus's natural way of infecting the body. Another method sometimes used is an aerosol spray into the nose. Vaccines for measles, influenza, and respiratory syncytial virus, an agent that causes the disease of childhood bronchiolitis, are sometimes given this way.

Only some vaccines give life-long protection. Others have to be repeated to remain effective.

Passive immunity occurs naturally when antibodies are transferred from a mother to her unborn baby.

AIDS: Killer Without a Cure

The virus that causes Acquired Immune Deficiency Syndrome (AIDS) has infected more than 60 million people since the early 1980s. Although the disease can be treated, there is still no cure, and roughly 25 million of those infected have died so far.

What is aids?

AIDS is caused by the human immunodeficiency virus (HIV). There are two types of AIDS virus, HIV-1 and 2, and a number of closely related ape viruses, the SIVs (simian immunodeficiency viruses). HIV infects white blood cells, attacking their natural processes and turning them over to virus production. During this process, the cells die, depriving the body of one of its defenses against infections.

A developing crisis

The AIDS crisis seems to have died down a little in the western world. If it cannot be cured, at least health awareness campaigns have kept the number of new infections down. The situation is very different in Africa, the probable home of the virus, and in much of Asia. Millions of Asians and Africans are dying from a disease that is now ranked as the fourth largest killer of the **microbe** world, taking more lives than malaria every year. Where did this killer disease come from?

AIDS is the cause of many millions of deaths in Africa and Asia.

Species hopping

In 1999 Dr. Beatrice H. Hahn and her team from the University of Alabama showed that HIV had probably passed from chimps to humans in West Africa in the 1950s. In 2006 another research team reported that they had found a virus very closely related to HIV in chimps in Cameroon, West Africa. Scientists now believe that the virus passed to humans several times, probably through injured hunters infected by chimp blood. It began to spread through humans in the 1950s, perhaps because of new medical practices, such as the use of hypodermic syringes. It may have spread from Africa after an infected traveler carried it to the United States.

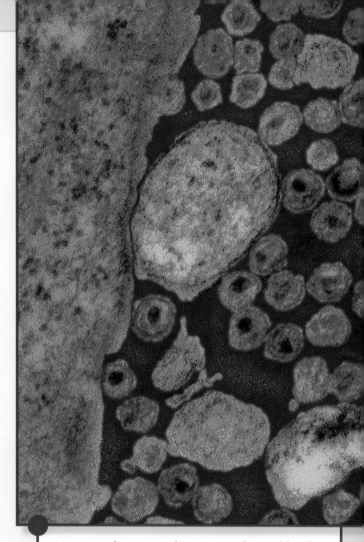

HIV can be passed on via infected body fluids, through sexual intercourse, blood tranfusion, or the reuse of infected syringes. Here the virus (red) is attacking the cell (green).

Shortened lives

In Botswana, Namibia, Swaziland, and Zimbabwe, between a fifth and a third of people between the ages of 15 and 49 have HIV or AIDS. Between a fifth and a half of women tested for the disease in Zimbabwe were carrying the virus. Because of AIDS, children born in these countries in the early years of the 21st century can expect to live for less than 40 years. Without the virus their life expectancy might have been closer to 70.

A moving target

HIV **mutates** and **evolves** rapidly. This makes it very difficult to come up with an effective treatment. HIV is like a moving target because it changes all the time. A further complication arises because there are different varieties of HIV—both of which may have originally come from a different ape or monkey species.

Rabies: The Fearsome Virus

Rabies is one of the most dreaded of all diseases. It is a virus disease of the central nervous system, the brain, and spinal cord, that afflicts warm-blooded animals, especially the dog family. It is transmitted to humans through contamination with the infected saliva of rabid animals. It is almost always fatal.

Pathway to the brain

The connection between rabies and the bite of a rabid animal has been known for centuries. The disease is caused by a virus that is concentrated in the saliva of the affected animal. It is transmitted by a bite, or a lick if the affected animal licks an open cut or wound. Once inside the body the virus travels along the nerves toward the central nervous system. Unlike many other disease agents it does not use the bloodstream as a means of transport.

The symptoms

Once infection has taken place, the time it takes for the symptoms to appear varies according to how badly the victim was bitten. It might take a year in some extreme cases. On average, symptoms appear about 30 days following a face bite, 40 days after an arm bite, and about 60 days after a leg bite.

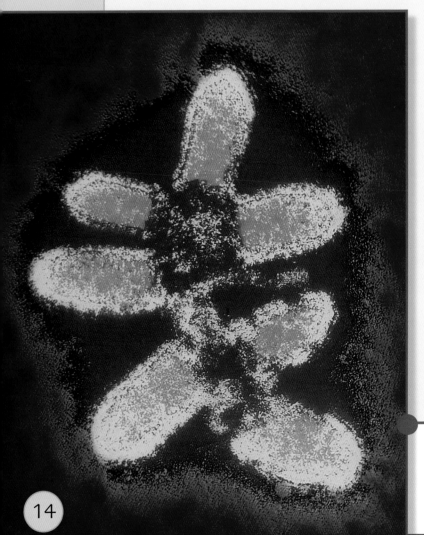

The deadly rabies virus, which is transmitted to humans by the bite of an infected animal.

Early symptoms include pain in the bite area, headache, slight fever, nausea, restlessness, anxiety, depression, and rapid speech. As the disease takes hold, restlessness, apprehension, and discomfort increase. Muscle spasms prevent the swallowing of food or water, although the victim will experience an intense thirst and become dehydrated. Death usually comes around the third day of this phase. Muscle spasms may occur at the mere sight or sound of water, explaining rabies' other name, hydrophobia, which means fear of water.

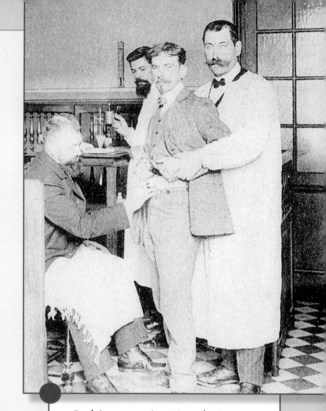

Rabies vaccination being carried out at the Pasteur Institute around 1910. The treatment at the time involved painful injections into the abdomen.

The treatment

Once symptoms develop, rabies is almost always fatal. There is no treatment that is guaranteed to succeed. The wounds must be washed thoroughly and then disinfected with carbolic or nitric acid if possible. An antirabies vaccine has greatly reduced the death rate from rabies, but it is not universally effective. Vaccinations must start at once, and five injections are given over the course of a month. Recently there has been success using an induced coma in a patient whose rabies symptoms had developed. Natural antibodies formed and the patient survived. Some people have a natural immunity to the virus and will not develop the disease.

Quarantine

Prevention appears to be better than cure as far as rabies is concerned. For example, strict **quarantine** laws have prevented the disease from crossing into Britain from Europe and have also kept it out of Australia. Quarantine works by preventing animals from entering a country until they have been tested and cleared of disease. It can be a very effective weapon against the spread of viruses and can also be used against human viruses.

Influenza: The Coming Epidemic?

In the years following World War One, the planet was struck by a virus **epidemic** that was more devastating, in terms of the number of deaths, than the plague of medieval times. It began on March 4, 1918, when the first case was reported in Kansas. Within four months, millions of people around the world had fallen ill. Few died of the disease, however, and most attention was focused on the approaching end of the war.

Killer switch

In September 1918, the relatively mild virus that had spread around the world changed into something that was much more deadly. In an almost simultaneous triple strike, the new **strain** hit France, Sierra Leone, and the city of Boston. Those infected died in large numbers, drowning as fluid filled their lungs. Appalled doctors thought that this strange new disease might be an airborne version of the Black Death. The virus spread rapidly. In six months, from September 1918 to March 1919, it killed more than 33,000 people in New York City alone. By the time the epidemic had run its course, an estimated 30 million people had died worldwide, many more than had been killed in the four years of fighting in the war. For some reason, still unknown, the virus was particularly dangerous among young adults.

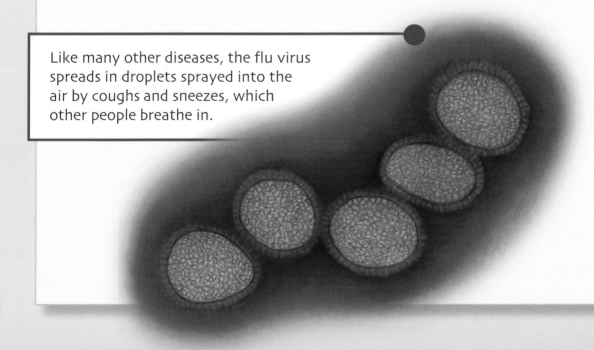

Like many other diseases, the flu virus spreads in droplets sprayed into the air by coughs and sneezes, which other people breathe in.

The cause of this epidemic was the influenza virus, although at the time no one knew that a virus caused flu. The 1918 strain of influenza persisted for a few years and then simply disappeared, or changed into a form that was not so **virulent**. Questions are still being asked as to what made this virus so deadly. Could it happen again?

New strains

Influenza epidemics occur when a new and highly virulent virus strain arises. Viruses change all the time. As they make billions of copies of themselves, mistakes are made. Some result in a weakened or non-functioning virus, while others may make it stronger.

Virus gene exchange

Viruses can also trade **genes** with each other and produce new strains. Humans have no immunity to these new strains, which are very different from the previous

The droplets expelled in a sneeze may carry viruses that can spread infectious diseases such as influenza.

strains. We actually increase the danger of new viruses emerging because of agricultural, industrial, and social practices. In 1997 a virulent form of bird flu, H5N1, began to infect small numbers of humans, mainly in southeast Asia. People who caught it, usually from working closely with farm birds, became seriously ill and many of them died. Although bird flu rarely transfers to humans, scientists have warned that if the bird flu virus is caught by someone who already has human flu, the two viruses could combine to make a new, very deadly strain of human flu. If this happens, it could cause a worldwide epidemic as bad as or worse than the 1918–1919 catastrophe.

Smallpox: A Disease Defeated

Smallpox has afflicted humans since prehistoric times. Caused by a virus, it is highly **contagious** and repeated **pandemics** have circled the world. It is often fatal and is characterized by high fever and a blistering rash, which usually leaves permanent scarring if the victim survives. In the 1700s it was a particular scourge in Europe and North America.

Edward Jenner

It was the search for an effective treatment for smallpox that led Edward Jenner to discover vaccination in 1796. Jenner discovered that he could safely give immunity from smallpox by vaccinating patients with matter from cowpox, a virus disease of cattle that is related to smallpox, but completely harmless to humans. Cowpox, or vaccinia in Latin, gave its name to the vaccination. Over the next century and a half variations on Jenner's procedure, using different vaccines, protected countless humans against bacterial diseases, such as typhoid, cholera, and tetanus, and viral illnesses, such as yellow fever and polio. Thanks to Jenner, smallpox became rarer and less virulent.

Smallpox symptoms

The incubation period of smallpox (the time from the introduction of the virus into the body to when symptoms start to show), is generally 11 to 12 days. The victim is highly contagious, especially when the rash develops. The virus is found on the skin, in the throat, and in the urine and feces. It may also survive on clothing and bedding. Infection can be spread through the air and by direct contact. There is no natural immunity to the disease—any non-vaccinated person exposed to smallpox will be infected by it. Babies are especially vulnerable to the disease.

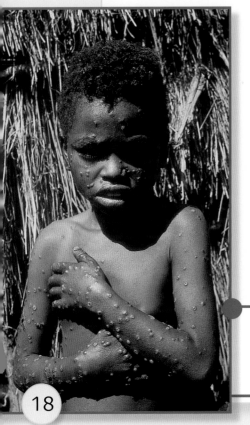

Smallpox was a terrible disease, producing a painful blistering rash on the skin of victims.

The early symptoms of smallpox are similar to those of influenza: high temperature, headache, muscle pains, chills, and sometimes vomiting. When the rash appears on about the fourth day, however, smallpox can be definitely diagnosed. The skin becomes sprinkled with spots and these become filled with fluid that is first clear, then becomes pus. In severe cases the spots leave permanent, disfiguring pockmarks.

The end of the disease

In 1967 the World Health Organization (WHO) of the United Nations began a worldwide program aimed at completely eradicating smallpox. Thirteen years later, after an intensive campaign of vaccination and quarantine, WHO announced that naturally-occurring smallpox had been totally eliminated from the world. The only deaths now caused by smallpox are isolated instances resulting from laboratory accidents. The last known case occurred in 1978.

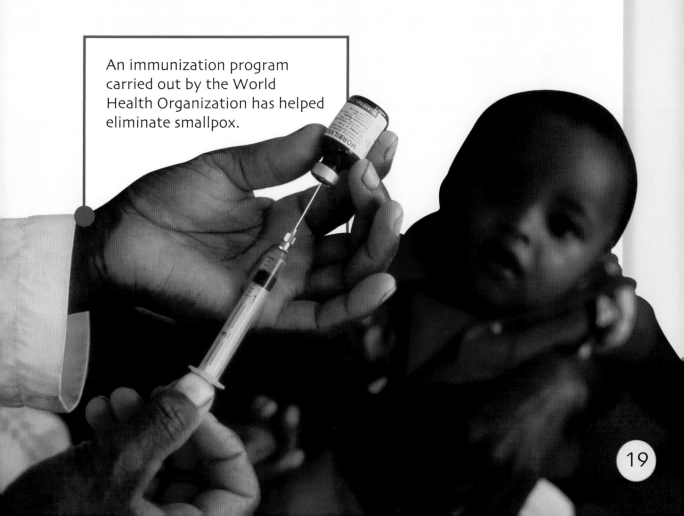

An immunization program carried out by the World Health Organization has helped eliminate smallpox.

Bacterial Diseases

We share our surroundings, and indeed our bodies, with a stunning number and variety of bacteria. There are more bacterial cells in and on your body than there are cells making you up! Fortunately, most of the bacteria are harmless, and some are even helpful.

Sizes and shapes

Bacteria can be shaped like rods (called bacilli), spheres (called cocci), or spirals (called spirilla), and vary in size from 40 to 800 millionths of an inch long, which makes them quite a bit bigger than viruses. Bacteria can be found as single cells or clusters of cells, or may form chains that can be either branched or straight. These differences in appearance are useful in classifying the different members of the bacterial kingdom.

Certain bacteria are able to form **spores**, which are extremely resistant to chemicals, heat, cold, or drying out. Bacteria grow and multiply in simple **nutrient** solutions, soils and natural waters, as well as in living organisms. Disease-causing bacteria grow in human organs and cause illness either by invading tissues or by producing **toxins** (poisons) that are harmful to certain organs or body functions. The symptoms of bacterial illness can range from mild uneasiness or brief illness to rapid death.

Number one killer

Tuberculosis, cholera, and tetanus are among the serious diseases caused by bacteria. Tuberculosis, indeed, is the number one cause of death by an infectious microbe.

Food poisoning

Food poisoning can be caused either by eating food containing bacterial toxins made in the food by bacteria, or by the growth in the body of bacteria that contaminated the food. *Staphylococcus aureus*, for example, can grow in dairy products that are not properly refrigerated. Vomiting and diarrhea occur a few hours after it is ingested. *Clostridium perfringens* grows in warm meat. Bacteria that get into the body produce spores in the intestines. This releases a toxin that causes diarrhea within a day of the contaminated food being consumed. *Salmonella* species may contaminate meat, poultry, and dairy products. The source of contamination is either the animal itself or the food handlers. If the food is not properly cooked before eating, the bacteria infect the intestinal tract and cause fever, vomiting, and diarrhea.

More bacteria

The most serious waterborne bacterial disease is cholera, caused by the bacterium *Vibrio cholerae*. Cholera poisons cause severe diarrhea that can result in the loss of 5 gallons (20 liters) of fluid per day and death by dehydration. Another bacterium, *Helicobacter pylori*, was only discovered in 1982. It lives in the lining of many people's stomachs and can cause stomach aches and stomach ulcers.

Bacteria are everywhere. This colony is growing on the tip of a hypodermic needle used to give shots.

Bacteria and Biofilms

Some bacteria can actually work together to form strong communities called **biofilms**. A biofilm consists of billions upon billions of microorganisms living on the surface of something that can provide the bacteria with water and nutrients. It is something like a microscopic city in which the bacteria are joined together to form a multicellular network.

Brush off the biofilm

If you reach into your mouth you may be able to touch a biofilm. The plaque that forms on your teeth if you do not brush regularly is a biofilm. Biofilms also form on poorly cleaned contact lenses and can lead to eye infections.

Slimes

When bacteria form biofilms, the cell walls of the individual bacteria become tougher and more difficult to penetrate. Biofilms are sometimes called slimes because the bacteria produce a coat of slimy material that helps protect them. A biofilm can be 1,500 times more resistant to **antibiotics** than a simple colony of bacteria. Some biofilms are even resistant to powerful chlorine-based disinfectants.

Pseudomonas aeruginosa

Pseudomonas aeruginosa is a common bacterium that forms biofilms. It can be found on fruit, vegetables, and in the soil. Individually, the cells can be controlled by antibiotics, but when they form biofilms they become much harder to fight and an infection can become untreatable and deadly. White blood cells, which could normally consume individual bacteria, can do nothing to attack a biofilm. One reason *Pseudomonas aeruginosa* is so much stronger in numbers is that when the bacteria get together, they release a kind of chemical signal. This tells the whole colony to make poisons that make them much more virulent and harder to kill. This kind of bacterial communication is called quorum sending.

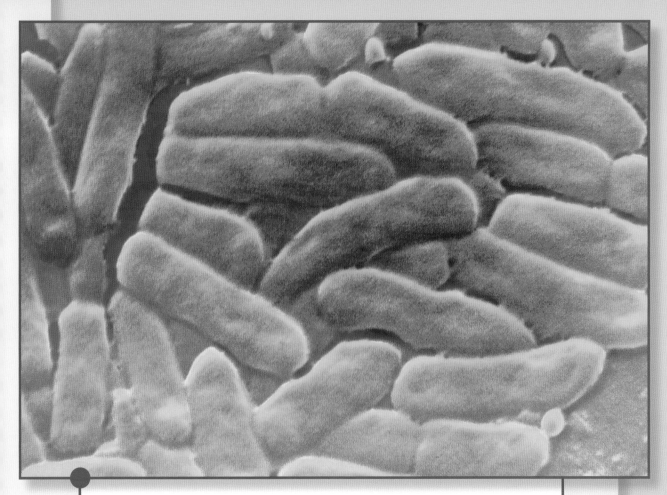

Pseudomonas aeruginosa is a bacterium that is found in hospitals, where it can infect people already weakened by illness or injury.

Signal blocking

Scientists are looking for ways to stop the formation of biofilms by disrupting the chemical conversations that go on between the bacteria when they are forming their network. The hope is that if the signaling process can be understood, then ways to block the signals can be developed. It is possible that by preventing the formation of biofilms, a way could be found to prevent dental plaque and other health problems.

Biofilm buddies

Biofilms are not all bad. Some are formed from harmless bacteria that line the insides of our intestines and give some protection from harmful disease-causing organisms.

Antibiotics

Antibiotics are substances that kill or restrict the growth of bacteria and fungi. They can be used to help the body fight infection from these microorganisms. Antibiotics have no effect on viruses.

Microscopic arms race

Antibiosis, which means "against life," is a term coined in the 19th century to describe a type of natural competition among different species of microbe. Antibiotics are produced naturally by various forms of bacteria and fungi as a way to gain an advantage in the competition for space and resources. When we use antibiotics we are simply making use of one microorganism's natural ways of attacking another.

Penicillin

Today, many different antibiotics are used to treat infections, and millions of lives have been saved since antibiotics were first used in 1941. Penicillin, the first antibiotic to be discovered (by Alexander Fleming in 1928), is perhaps still the best known. It is named after *Penicillium notatum*, the mold that produces it. We now have a number of other antibiotics, all of which are effective against different bacterial and fungal diseases.

The growing resistance

People are becoming concerned because many disease-causing bacteria are becoming resistant to

Penicillium molds are the most widespread and will colonize exposed foods. This mold is growing on a tomato.

the effects of antibiotics. Although antibiotic-resistant bacteria are not yet widespread in the general population, they are becoming more common in hospitals, especially in patients who have been treated with many drugs over a long period of time. Many patients do not finish their courses of antibiotics because they feel better before they finish the treatment. This leaves some bacteria alive, and these bacteria are the ones most likely to pass resistance to the antibiotic on to the next generation of bacteria.

The next generation

Scientists are working to develop a new generation of antibiotics to treat the growing number of resistant bacteria. However, it seems likely that the bacteria will continue to evolve and adapt to whatever we throw at them. Many doctors now think that antibiotic use should be restricted. They blame over-prescription of antibiotics in the past, saying that this has given bacteria the opportunity to develop resistance. Resistance to an antibiotic can spread swiftly through a population of bacteria because they have the ability to exchange genetic material and pass resistance on to each other.

Scientists are working constantly to develop new treatments to fight bacteria that become resistant to present-day antibiotics.

Antibiotics in farming

The widespread use of antibiotics in farm animals has also helped the spread of drug-resistant bacteria. Farmers began feeding animals antibiotics to promote growth and prevent infection. Inevitably the bacteria in the animals became more drug-resistant and this has led to hazards, such as the appearance of drug-resistant *Salmonella*, one of the causes of food poisoning. *Salmonella* is spread through eating incompletely cooked meat, poultry, or eggs.

Tuberculosis: Return of a Killer

Tuberculosis (TB) is caused by a bacterium called *Mycobacterium tuberculosis*. The symptoms are coughs, weight loss, night sweats, fever, chest pains, and coughing up blood. Tuberculosis spreads through airborne droplets sprayed out whenever an infected person coughs. These can remain in the air for roughly two hours then breathed in by someone else who will be infected.

The forgotten disease

Tuberculosis is a disease that has largely been forgotten in the major industrialized countries of the world. It is often thought of as something that happened in the past. In the early 1800s, it caused many deaths. TB kills by eating away at body tissues, such as the lungs, until they no longer work. Long ago, however, people did not understand how TB was spread. It was once believed that tuberculosis was caused when people got too emotional!

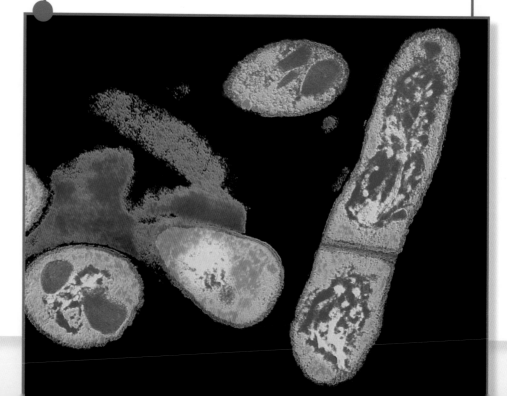

Mycobacterium tuberculosis, the cause of tuberculosis in humans. New drug-resistant strains of the bacterium are bringing the return of a disease that was once thought to have been largely eradicated.

The antibiotic answer

In 1865 Jean Antoine Villemin demonstrated scientifically that tuberculosis was an infectious illness and, in 1882, Robert Koch identified *Mycobacterium tuberculosis* as the disease agent. Once it was discovered that tuberculosis was contagious, measures were taken to prevent its spread. Infected people were isolated in sanatoriums. Living conditions were improved in towns and cities. In 1908 the BCG vaccination was developed and gave children immunity from the disease. By the middle years of the 1900s, effective antibiotics that treated and cured most cases had been developed. Across Europe and the United States tuberculosis was being defeated—or so it seemed.

TB on the rise

In the mid-1980s, the number of reported tuberculosis infections began to increase steadily around the world. One important cause has been the emergence of new forms, or strains, of the original bacterium that are resistant to most of the drugs once used to treat it. This is sometimes called MDR-TB, or multiple drug resistant tuberculosis. Around the world tuberculosis kills between 2 and 3 million people every year, more than any other infectious disease. In March 1998, the World Health Organization issued a warning that TB could infect 1 billion more people in the next 20 years and that 70 million of them are likely to die.

Fighting back

Some progress has been made against tuberculosis, and scientists are working to develop a drug that is effective against the new resistant TB strains. TB, however, attracts fewer resources than many other diseases. The reason, unfortunately, is that it tends to be a disease of the poor—malnourished people have less resistance to the disease. As people in the drug industry have admitted, the people in the most affected areas are those least able to pay for treatment. The rise of international air travel makes it difficult to stop the spread of the disease.

Infectious Fungi

Fungi will grow on any wet material, whether it is indoors or outdoors. It will even grow on moist parts of the human body. Fungi can cause disease in three ways. They can produce an allergic reaction in sensitive individuals; they produce poisons called mycotoxins; and they can invade and grow in or on the body.

Mycosis

The growth of a fungus on or in the body is called **mycosis**. Fungal infections often take hold after the use of antibiotics. These drugs get rid of the body's harmless bacteria as well as the disease-causing varieties, and this leaves a "space" for fungal or other invaders to fill. The immune system of normally healthy people is powerful enough to prevent invasion by nearly all fungi.

Many fungal infections affect only the outer layers of skin, and although they are annoying and sometimes difficult to cure, they are not life-threatening. Athlete's foot is a common fungal infection, but perhaps the best-known of the infectious fungi are the candida yeasts. These can grow and become a problem in the digestive or urinary tracts of the body.

Internal infections

Fungi that affect the deeper layers of skin and internal organs can cause serious, sometimes fatal, illness. *Cryptococcus* is a type of fungus that can cause a form of meningitis, an inflammation of the meninges (the membrane that encloses the brain). For some reason it affects men twice as often as women. It can also affect the lungs, causing coughs and fever, or spread to the nervous system. There is no reliable treatment for this infection and it is usually fatal. *Cryptococcus neoformans*, the disease agent, has been found in pigeon droppings.

Sporotrichosis is an infection found in those who come into regular contact with plants and soil, such as farmers. The disease affects the skin and lymphatic system. It is rarely fatal.

Histoplasmosis

Histoplasmosis is a severe fungal infection that can cause a wide variety of symptoms. In acute cases ulcers form inside the throat, and the liver and **spleen** become enlarged. In other forms of the infection, the lungs can become damaged and develop injuries similar to those caused by tuberculosis. Sometimes no disease symptoms are apparent at all and the infection is usually discovered accidentally when the chest is X-rayed.

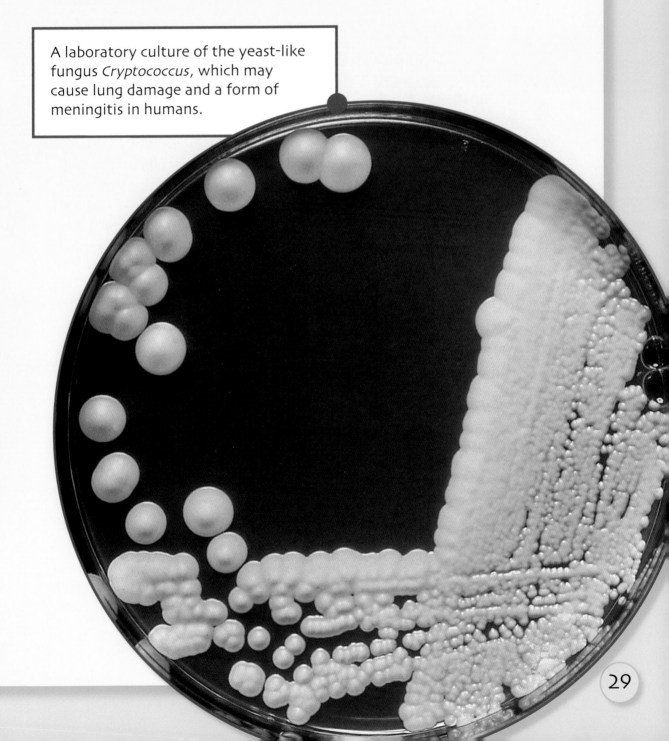

A laboratory culture of the yeast-like fungus *Cryptococcus*, which may cause lung damage and a form of meningitis in humans.

Protistan Parasites

The protists are single-celled life forms that occur in a great variety of shapes and sizes, ranging from 80 to 4,000 millionths of an inch. One of the best known, and deadliest, protists are the group of four *Plasmodium* species that cause malaria. *Plasmodium's* complex life cycle, which we will examine later, involves multi-stage development in humans, coupled with further development in the gut of a female mosquito.

Leishmaniasis

Other problem protists include the Leishmania species. Dogs and rodents act as a reservoir for the parasites. They are transmitted to humans by the bite of female sandflies, which pick up the infection when they bite animals. Leishmaniasis takes many forms, from self-healing ulcers to terrible destruction of facial features when the parasites invade the membranes of the nose and mouth. One feature of the Leishmania parasites that makes them difficult to deal with is that they actually invade the white blood cells that are normally responsible for dealing with microbe invaders. More than 12 million people are afflicted with this disease.

The black sickness

The most dangerous form of leishmaniasis is commonly referred to as kala-azar, a Hindi term meaning "black sickness." The name describes the increased discoloring of the skin that is typical of the disease. If left untreated, kala-azar is invariably fatal.

Sleeping sickness

African trypanosomiasis, or "sleeping sickness," is caused by a type of parasite called a trypanosome. These trypanosomes are transmitted to humans by the bite of tsetse flies. Initial symptoms include fever, headache, dizziness, and weakness. Later, when the parasites invade the central nervous system, hallucinations, delusions, and seizures affect the victim. If untreated the patient may lapse into a coma and eventually die. This disease affects some 25,000 people every year.

Master of disguise

An intriguing feature of the sleeping sickness trypanosome is its ability to repeatedly change the protein that covers its surface. By doing this it tricks the victim's immune system and keeps it from identifying the parasite and producing antibodies against it. The complex genetic mechanism that allows the parasite to do this is not yet understood.

A tsetse fly on a person's arm. The insect is the carrier of the parasitic trypanosome that causes sleeping sickness in humans.

Malaria: The Efficient Killer

Every 12 seconds someone in the world dies from malaria—that is 2.7 million people every year, and most of them are children under five. Up to 500 million people are infected at any one time. The cause of this terrible disease is a parasitic protist called *Plasmodium*.

Mosquitoes and malaria

The vector for malaria is the Anopheles mosquito. The female mosquito sucks blood by inserting her proboscis (the insect's slender feeding tube) into her victim's skin. As she does so her saliva is injected into the human's bloodstream. If the mosquito is infected with *Plasmodium* the saliva will contain thousands of tiny thread-like parasites called sporozoites.

A complex life cycle

The sporozoites make their way to the liver, where they form spores in the liver cells and begin to multiply. Two weeks later,

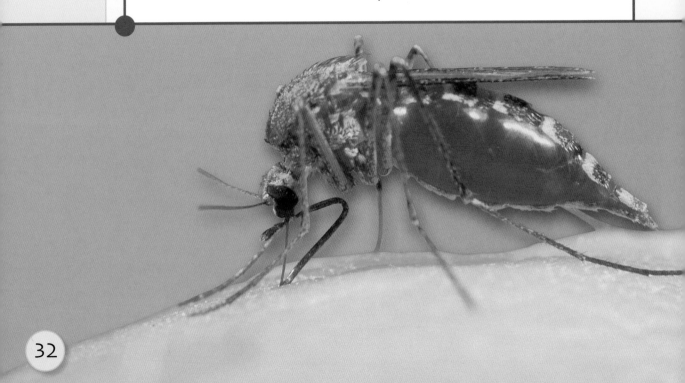

The female Anopheles mosquito is the carrier of the *Plasmodium* parasite that is the cause of malaria. The parasite is transmitted to the human victim when the mosquito bites.

the liver cells burst, releasing large numbers of spores, now called merozoites, into the bloodstream. When this happens the sufferer begins to feel very ill, with weakness, tiredness, fever, aches, and pains. Each merozoite attacks and invades a red blood cell, feeding and growing inside it until it is half the size of the cell. Then, it splits into 24 new merozoites that burst the blood cell apart and emerge to attack new blood cells. Up to 70 percent of the victim's red blood cells could be colonized by the parasite.

Hitching a ride

Some of the merozoites separate into male and female stages called gametocytes and migrate to blood vessels in the skin where they wait for a female mosquito to return. When the mosquito feeds, she sucks up a mouthful of gametocytes. The gametocytes breed in the mosquito's intestines and form cysts that embed themselves in the intestinal wall. Two or three weeks later, thousands of little sporozoites burst out of the cysts and make their way into the mosquito's salivary gland, where they are ready to infect another human with the mosquito's next bite.

Plasmodium evasions

Plasmodium has adapted itself very efficiently for life in its human and mosquito hosts. It manages to evade the body's defenses with ease. Once injected by the mosquito's saliva, the parasites take only half an hour to get inside the liver cells. This isn't enough time for the antibodies in the bloodstream to attack and kill them all. The next line of defense is the killer T cells, part of the immune system, which hunt down and kill cells that have been invaded. The trouble is that it takes 10 to 12 days for this response to kick in. Before this happens, the parasite leaves the liver cells and attacks the red blood cells, and red blood cells do not trigger the T cell response.

Plasmodium is always one step ahead. As the parasites develop inside the red blood cells, they produce tiny knobs on the surface of the cells that cause the infected red blood cells to stick to the lining of the smallest blood vessels. The result is that the infected red blood cells are kept out of the spleen, which would recognize them as damaged cells and destroy them.

Malaria: The Search for a Solution

Malaria infections are not permanent. The most serious of the malarial strains will kill up to half the people it infects if left untreated. Those who survive will eventually rid themselves of the disease over a period of three to five years. Unfortunately, if they live in a malaria-infected area, they are likely to become reinfected. Roughly one-third of the world's population live in malarial areas. This means millions of people live in a perpetually weakened condition, with their resistance to other infections seriously reduced.

False hopes

For a few decades after World War Two, malaria seemed to be on the retreat. Quinine, derived from the bark of the cinchona tree, and chloroquine, a similar **synthetic compound**, were effective treatments. DDT insecticide sprays were used to kill the mosquito that carried the *Plasmodium* parasite. Then nature caught up—the parasite and mosquito became immune to the chemicals being thrown at them. Malaria came back stronger than before. There were three times as many cases of malaria in the 1990s as there had been in the 1960s.

Searching for a vaccine

Immunologists trying to find a vaccine to defeat malaria find themselves facing many problems. Unlike a virus or a bacterium, which more or less stay the same, the malaria parasite goes through four stages of development in a human (see pages 32–33). A vaccine that is effective against the sporozoites might have no effect on the liver or blood stages, for example. In addition, an anti-malaria vaccine would have to be extraordinarily efficient. It takes just one or two sporozoites to survive to produce tens of thousands of merozoites in the liver.

Weakened parasites

A possible solution would be to create a vaccine of weakened parasites, but this is not easy. The sporozoites will only grow inside mosquitoes. The liver stages only live inside human liver cells, and the merozoites live in red blood cells.

It is difficult for researchers to get enough of the parasites to work on. One option that seems to work is to take a mosquito infected with sporozoites and dose it with **radiation**. The parasites inside the mosquito are weakened by this treatment. Once in the human bloodstream they will still travel to the liver, but they will not produce merozoites and colonize the red blood cells. They remain in the liver where they trigger a response from the immune system. The next time a healthy malaria parasite gets into the blood, the immune system is geared up and ready to deal with it.

DNA vaccine

Recently tests have been carried out using a "**DNA** vaccine." This involves injecting a person with the gene that makes the sporozoite's protective protein coat. There is more about DNA vaccines on page 44. The effect is to trigger the production of antibodies that will attack living sporozoites. However, a reliable vaccine still seems a distant prospect.

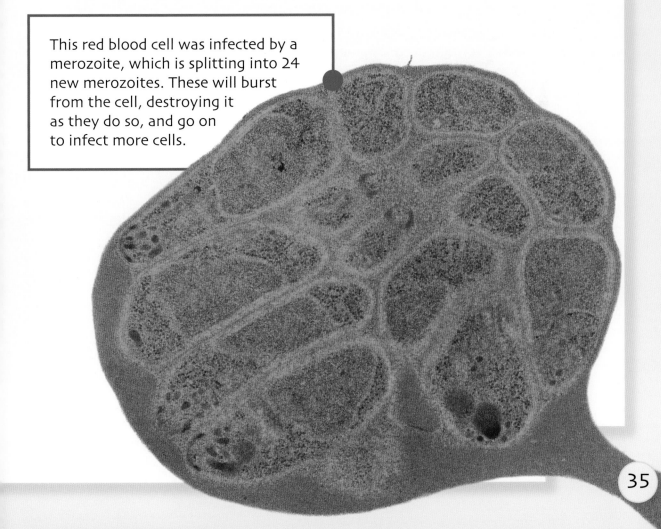

This red blood cell was infected by a merozoite, which is splitting into 24 new merozoites. These will burst from the cell, destroying it as they do so, and go on to infect more cells.

Helminth Horrors

The largest and most complex of the infectious disease agents are the multicellular helminths. These have complex life cycles that may involve microscopic eggs and larvae and larger adult stages. The helminths include many types of parasitic worms.

The most common parasite?

Ascaris worms are probably the most common parasite in the world. They are found in temperate as well as tropical regions. Infection can cause abdominal pain and a lack of weight gain in children. It can sometimes result in a dangerous obstruction in the intestines.

Tapeworms

The tapeworm causes serious disease. Usually, people are infected by eating undercooked pork that contains the larval form of the parasite. The larvae develop into adult worms in the victim's intestine. Eggs leave the body in the feces and may be eaten by pigs to continue the parasite's life cycle. When eggs are inadvertently eaten by people, the larvae may infect the central nervous system, causing serious disorders, including seizures. This disease is a serious problem in some rural parts of Latin America.

The biggest disease agent

Intestinal tapeworms are the largest of all disease agents, growing to lengths of 10 to 33 feet (3 to 10 meters) in human intestines.

Blood flukes

Schistosomiasis, a major disease that affects more than 200 million people in Africa, Asia, and South America, is caused by blood flukes, a type of flatworm. Roughly 200,000 people die every year, and many more (about 10 percent of those infected) suffer damage to vital organs such as the liver and kidneys.

Snail vector

Schistosomiasis is interesting because it is not transmitted through the bite of an insect. The larvae develop within fresh-water snails. After leaving the snail, the larvae swim along until they contact a human host who is bathing or working in the water. They penetrate the skin, then migrate through the blood vessels. Adult flukes 0.2 to 0.8 inches (6 to 20 millimeters) long take up residence in the veins of the intestine, liver, or bladder, depending on the parasite species. The adult male and female worms pair, mate, and produce large numbers of eggs. Some of the eggs they release become lodged in the organs, causing scar tissue to form. This scar tissue can block blood vessels, causing them to **rupture**. This can prove fatal. Eggs that are shed in feces or urine enter the water and develop into larvae living inside fresh-water snails. They then exit the snails and enter the water, where they swim until they find a human to start the cycle again.

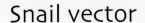

A tapeworm, showing the suckers with which it attaches itself to the lining of the intestines.

Microbe Mutations

One of the things that can make infectious diseases so hard to deal with is the speed with which they can change. Like the rest of the living world, bacteria and viruses are constantly evolving. The difference is that a generation for a bacterium might be just 20 minutes. This is like you having great grandchildren within an hour of being born. This rapid turnover allows resistant strains to emerge quickly.

Mutations

A mutation is a change in the genetic material, or genes, of an organism. It can happen when a cell's DNA is copied before the cell divides. Sometimes mistakes are made when the DNA is replicated. Some mutations are of no consequence, and so are never noticed. Others are disastrous and the mutant organism does not survive.

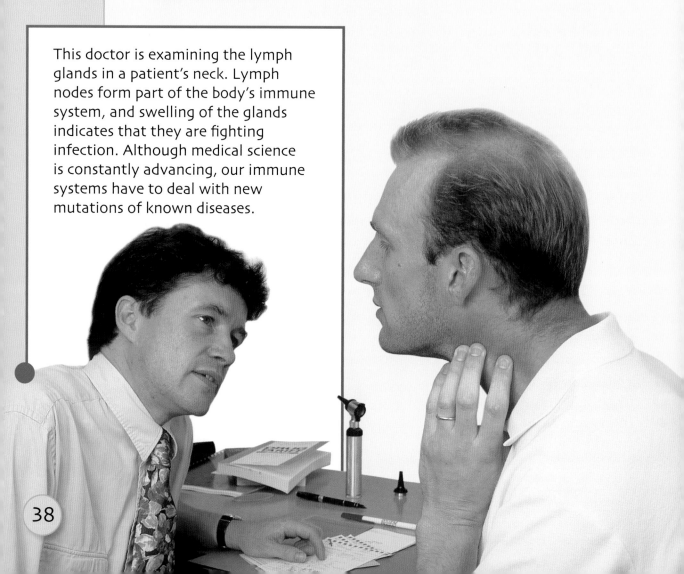

This doctor is examining the lymph glands in a patient's neck. Lymph nodes form part of the body's immune system, and swelling of the glands indicates that they are fighting infection. Although medical science is constantly advancing, our immune systems have to deal with new mutations of known diseases.

Every now and then, however, a mutation occurs that gives the organism an advantage, something that makes it better able to survive in its environment. When this happens, the organism can pass on the advantage to the next generation.

Sharing good fortune

Bacteria can sometimes share their good mutations with other bacteria they happen to meet. Resistance to an antibiotic, for example, can be passed from bacterium to bacterium by way of circular pieces of DNA called **plasmids**.

Staying the course

Unwittingly we often help the strongest strains to survive. If you have a bacterial infection you will be infected by both strong and weak strains of the bacteria. Taking a series of antibiotics will wipe out the weaker bacteria first and the more resistant strains will fill the gaps. If you do not finish the course of treatment—and many people don't—the toughest bacteria survive. When they go on to infect someone else they will be much harder to destroy.

An epidemic of resistance

By 1993 it was determined that nearly every common disease-causing bacterial species had developed some degree of drug resistance. More than two dozen of these emergent strains were potentially life-threatening and resistant to most commonly available antibiotic treatments. One scientist called it "an epidemic of microbial resistance."

Mutant traveler

A single mutant bacterium can give rise to a strain that spreads over the world within just a few years. In the 1970s a *Streptococcus* infection struck children in hospitals in South Africa. When the bacterial strain was analyzed it matched one that had been discovered in a remote village in New Guinea 10 years earlier. How it reached South Africa remains a mystery, but eventually it made it all around the world.

Emerging Diseases

Emerging diseases are those that are new to us, those that are reappearing after a period of decline, and those that are developing resistance to drugs. The emerging infectious diseases include all major types of disease agents.

Defining diseases

New diseases become known to us through the symptoms they produce. When someone gets sick, doctors decide what the disease is from the symptoms they see. If the symptoms match no known disease they might indicate that a new disease is at work, and a new disease agent has to be identified.

Making an identification

The usual method of identifying a microbe is by taking blood and tissue samples and trying to grow the microbe in the laboratory. Microscopic examination and a variety of tests are then carried out to identify it. Many disease agents, though, cannot be grown. Because they are unknown organisms, no one knows what conditions they need to grow. Others simply cannot exist outside the body.

A researcher at the U.S. Centers for Disease Control (CDC) in Atlanta, Georgia.

On the front line

Hundreds of cases of unexplained illness can be under investigation at any one time. Powerful new technologies are used to identify microbes by examining their genetic material. There is always the possibility that one of these unknown agents could emerge as the next HIV, or a deadly strain of influenza. New disease agents identified since 1975 have included Ebola, Hanta, and HIV. Diseases once thought to have been defeated, such as tuberculosis, are reappearing in new antibiotic-resistant forms.

Legionnaire's disease

In 1976 people attending an American Legion convention in Philadelphia started getting sick. Doctors suspected at first that the cause was swine flu. CDC researchers worked for eight months before they realized that the cause was actually a previously unknown bacterium. The new disease was called Legionnaire's disease, after its first identified victims. The bacterium invades the body in inhaled water droplets, and often causes outbreaks when it contaminates water supplies or air-conditioning systems.

A researcher in a biologically secure laboratory at the Harvard Medical School. Here, dangerous viruses, such as HIV, are studied.

Superbugs

Since the 1960s, increasing numbers of people have died from being infected with "superbugs" in hospitals. These are dangerous bacteria that have become resistant to antibiotics (see pages 38–39). The best known is MRSA (methicillin-resistant *Staphylococcus aureus*). These are *Staphylococcus aureus* bacteria that are resistant to the antibiotic methicillin and most other antibiotics. MRSA is common and many people carry it on their skin. However, when it infects the very sick or elderly in hospitals, or invades the body through unclean equipment, it can cause deadly blood poisoning or pneumonia. MRSA infections are on the increase and now kill thousands every year.

Spreading fast

With the speed of travel around the world today diseases can spread with terrifying rapidity. An influenza epidemic like the one that caused so many deaths between 1918 and 1919 would spread around the world in four days rather than four months. It is next to impossible to predict what new diseases we will have to face during the 21st century.

DNA Vaccines: The Shape of Things to Come?

Vaccination is an important weapon in the war against bacteria and viruses. Traditional vaccines consist of either weakened or heat-killed viruses, or use proteins from the virus's protein coat to trigger the immune system. Anti-bacterial vaccines are made from bacterial toxins or from sugars found in the cell walls of the bacteria.

Targeting genes

Vaccines have obviously been successful but they do not work against all disease agents. A vaccine might be effective against one strain of a virus but not another. Scientists are now working on vaccines that make use of the disease agent's genes.

Genes and proteins

A gene is part of an organism's hereditary, or genetic, material. Each gene is like a code or set of instructions for making a protein. Proteins are large and complex molecules that perform a number of vital tasks in an organism, from controlling the rate of chemical reactions to providing structural support.

Dr. Yen Choo of the Laboratory of Molecular Biology in Cambridge, England has helped to develop a technique that could "turn off" the gene that causes leukemia.

In 1990 scientists discovered that genes from other organisms could be absorbed by cells in the body to produce proteins. A gene from a disease agent can be inserted into a circular piece of DNA called a plasmid. When this DNA plasmid is injected into someone, the DNA serves as a blueprint for the production of the disease agent protein. Because the DNA vaccine only has the code for a small part of the disease agent, it cannot become infectious.

Immune trigger

It is believed that because the disease agent's protein originates inside the host cells, it triggers antibody production by the immune system. This immune response is in some respects superior to that produced by traditional vaccines and gives better protection against viral infections.

A cure for flu?

Much of the work on DNA vaccines has focused on producing an effective vaccine against influenza. Traditional anti-influenza vaccines have targeted proteins on the surface of the virus particle. However, these proteins change frequently as the genes that produce them mutate. The DNA vaccine being developed targets a protein inside the virus that is much less likely to change. DNA vaccines may also be used to treat people who are already suffering from viral infections, such as hepatitis or HIV. By boosting the immune response using a DNA vaccine, some scientists believe the immune system could be enhanced enough to kill all the infected cells and wipe out the infection.

The risks

The development of a DNA vaccine against HIV, the virus that causes AIDS, is a possibility. The safety of DNA vaccines is being carefully monitored by researchers. One concern is whether or not the injected DNA will become incorporated into the patient's **chromosomes**, although there is no evidence so far that it does. There is also a possibility that a DNA vaccine would cause the body's immune system to attack its own cells because they are making foreign proteins. However, DNA vaccines could be the treatment of tomorrow.

Biological Weapons

Perhaps no form of warfare has been more rightly condemned than the threat to use disease agents deliberately as a weapon. Biological agents of warfare are living organisms, whatever their nature, intended to cause disease or death.

The effects of biological agents vary greatly, depending on the properties of the disease-causing microorganisms, the method of transmitting the agent to people, and how susceptible the people are to the disease. Depending on which organism is used, there may be a delay of a few days to a few weeks before any effect is seen. The result of an attack would also depend on how contagious the agent is.

Potential weapons

Viruses, bacteria, and fungi can all be used as biological weapons. They could be used against humans, domestic animals, or plants. To be useful for biological warfare, the microorganisms would have to be relatively easy to grow in the laboratory. They must be able to survive in air for several hours or in water or food for several days, and they must cause severe, but not necessarily fatal, illness for a long time. The viral diseases influenza, yellow fever, and dengue fever and the bacterial diseases anthrax, plague, and dysentery all meet these demands for attacks on humans.

Deploying the disease

Biological weapons have often been regarded as cheap and simple substitutes for nuclear or chemical weapons for use against populations in large areas. Spray devices mounted on aircraft or ships could be used to release the weapon. Large areas could be covered using equipment like this. In theory a single aircraft spraying a deadly organism could kill half the people in an area the size of New York City. Another method would be to infect a city's water supply.

No protection

The most efficient protection against a biological weapon would be vaccination, but since this would have to be carried out weeks or months in advance of an attack, and as there would be no knowledge of the type of organism to be used, it is not a realistic option.

In 1972 an international convention forbade the production, storage, and use of biological weapons. However, it was not considered a guarantee against the development of biological weapons, because there were few controls and many ways in which research and production of biological agents could be hidden. Within only a few years there were a number of allegations that the treaty had been broken. Recently the possibility of using genetic engineering (deliberately changing the genetic material of an organism) to produce powerful and dangerous new biological weapons has emerged.

Big cities practice what they would do if they were attacked by biological weapons. Here, members of the response team wear protective suits and are given a decontamination shower.

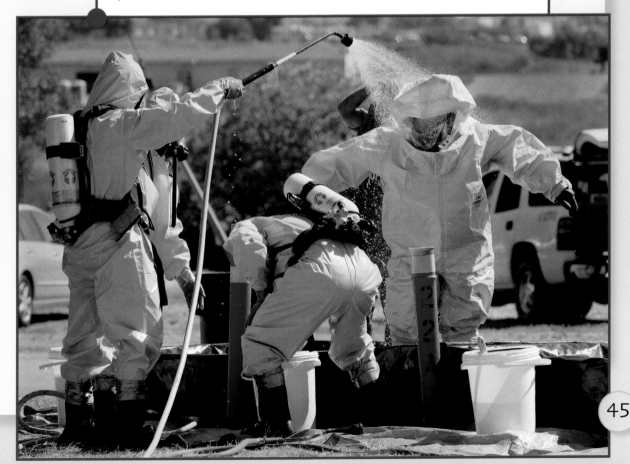

Glossary

antibiotic substance produced by or obtained from certain bacteria or fungi that can be used to kill or inhibit the growth of disease-causing microorganisms

antibody defensive protein produced by an organism in response to the presence of foreign or invading substances such as the proteins found on viruses or bacteria

bacterium (plural bacteria) any of a large group of single-celled organisms that have no organized nucleus

biofilm colony of billions of bacteria living on a surface that can provide them with water and nutrients. The biofilm colony produces a protective slimy coat.

cell the basic unit of life. Cells can exist as independent life forms, such as bacteria and protists, or form tissues in more complicated life forms, such as muscle cells and nerve cells in animals.

chromosome thread-like structures that become visible in the nucleus of a cell just before it divides. Chromosomes carry the genes that determine the characteristics of an organism.

compound substance formed from two or more chemical elements

contagious describes a disease that can be transmitted by contact between one organism and another

disease agent organism, such as a bacterium, that can cause disease

DNA (deoxyribonuleic acid) genetic material of almost all living things with the exception of some viruses. DNA consists of two long chains of nucleotides joined together in a double helix.

epidemic disease that affects many people at the same time and spreads rapidly by infection

evolve in biology, to develop a characteristic over a period of time as a result of mutation and natural selection

fungus (plural fungi) any of a group of spore-producing organisms, such as mushrooms and molds

gene unit of heredity. A gene is a length of DNA and a number of genes are carried on a chromosome. A gene is the set of instructions for assembling a protein from amino acids.

helminth any of a group of parasitic worms, such as flukes and tapeworms

immune system cells of the body that give protection against invasion by foreign microorganisms such as bacteria and viruses. These include cells that directly attack invading organisms and cells that destroy infected body cells.

immunization giving immunity to a disease by introducing a weakened or killed form of a virus into the body. This triggers the immune system's response to that disease, making it ready to deal effectively with the active form of the virus if encountered.

infectious describes something that is capable of causing infection or is caused by an infection (an infection is an invasion of an organism by disease-causing microorganisms)

interferon protein produced by cells in the body that are infected by viruses. It travels to other non-infected cells and helps to protect them from infection.

microbe another name for a microorganism

microorganism any microscopic living thing, such as bacteria and protists

mutation change in the genes produced by a change in DNA as it is copied during cell division. Most mutations are harmful to the organism.

mycosis growth of a fungus on or in the body

nutrient any nutritious substance found in food

pandemic epidemic that is spread over a wide geographical area

parasite one organism living on another and benefiting at the expense of it

plasmid circular strand of DNA found in bacteria that is separate from the main chromosome DNA

protein one of a group of complex organic molecules that perform a variety of essential tasks in living things, including providing structure and controlling the rates of chemical reactions

protist any single-celled eukaryote that is a member of the kingdom Protista

quarantine period of time during which a person or animal suspected of carrying an infectious disease is kept isolated to prevent the spread of the disease

radiation energy transmitted in the form of waves or particles as a result of the breakdown of a radioactive substance

rupture to break open or burst

spleen organ of the body; part of its job is to destroy old or damaged red blood cells

spore resting state of a bacterium, entered when conditions are unfavorable. A spore can resist hostile conditions for long periods of time.

strain group of organisms of one species that have distinctive characteristics but are not sufficiently different to be considered a separate species

symptom any change in mind or body that indicates that someone is suffering from a disease

synthetic describes something that is produced by artificial means rather than naturally

toxin poisonous substance produced by an organism, such as a bacterium

vaccination giving a vaccine in order to give protection from a disease

vaccine weakened or killed form of a bacterium or virus that causes disease, given to stimulate the immune system to produce antibodies against the disease

vector path by which a disease-causing microorganism travels from one host to another. Biting insects are a common vector of disease.

virulent describes the disease-causing ability of a microorganism

virus infective particle, usually consisting of a molecule of nucleic acid in a protein coat

Further Research

More Books to Read

Claybourne, Anna. *Science Answers: Microlife*. Chicago: Heinemann, 2004.

Parker, Steve. *Microlife That Helps Us*. Chicago: Raintree, 2006.

Ward, Brian. *Microscopic Life in Your Food*. North Mankato, Minn.: Smart Apple Media, 2004.

Using the Internet

Explore the Internet to find out more about infectious diseases. You can use a search engine, such as www.google.com, and type in keywords such as *rabies, infectious fungi,* or *malaria*. These search tips will help you find useful websites more quickly:

* Know exactly what you want to find out about first.

* Use only a few important keywords in a search, putting the most relevant words first.

* Be precise. Only use names of people, places, or things.

Index